Adult Coloring Book
Madalas Relaxation Coloring

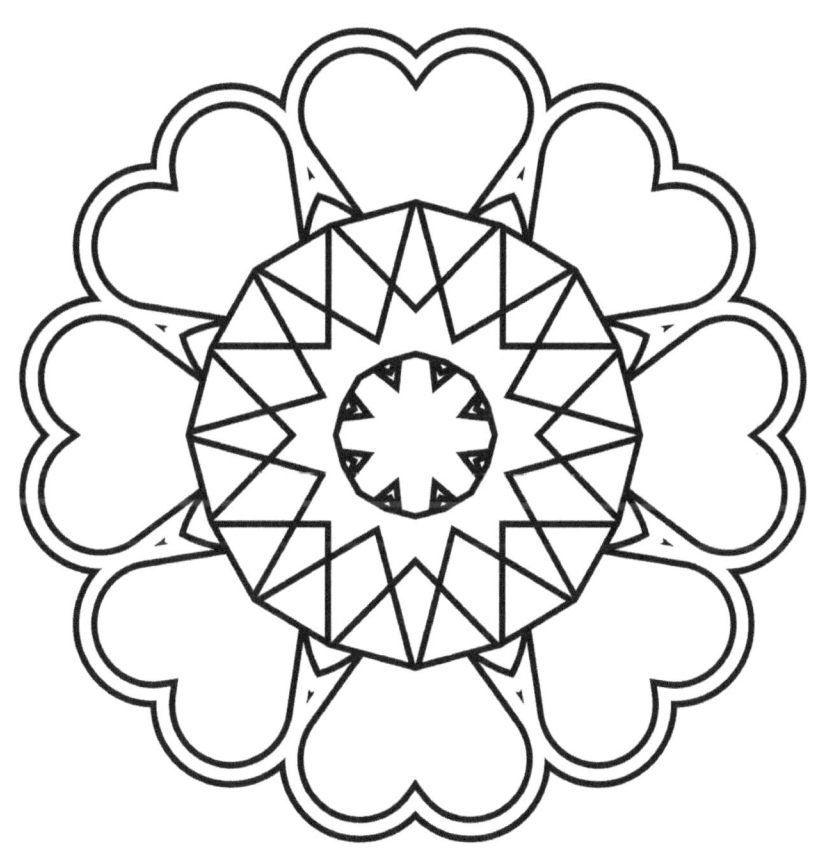

Belinda L. Frazier

Adult Coloring Book
Madalas Relaxation Coloring

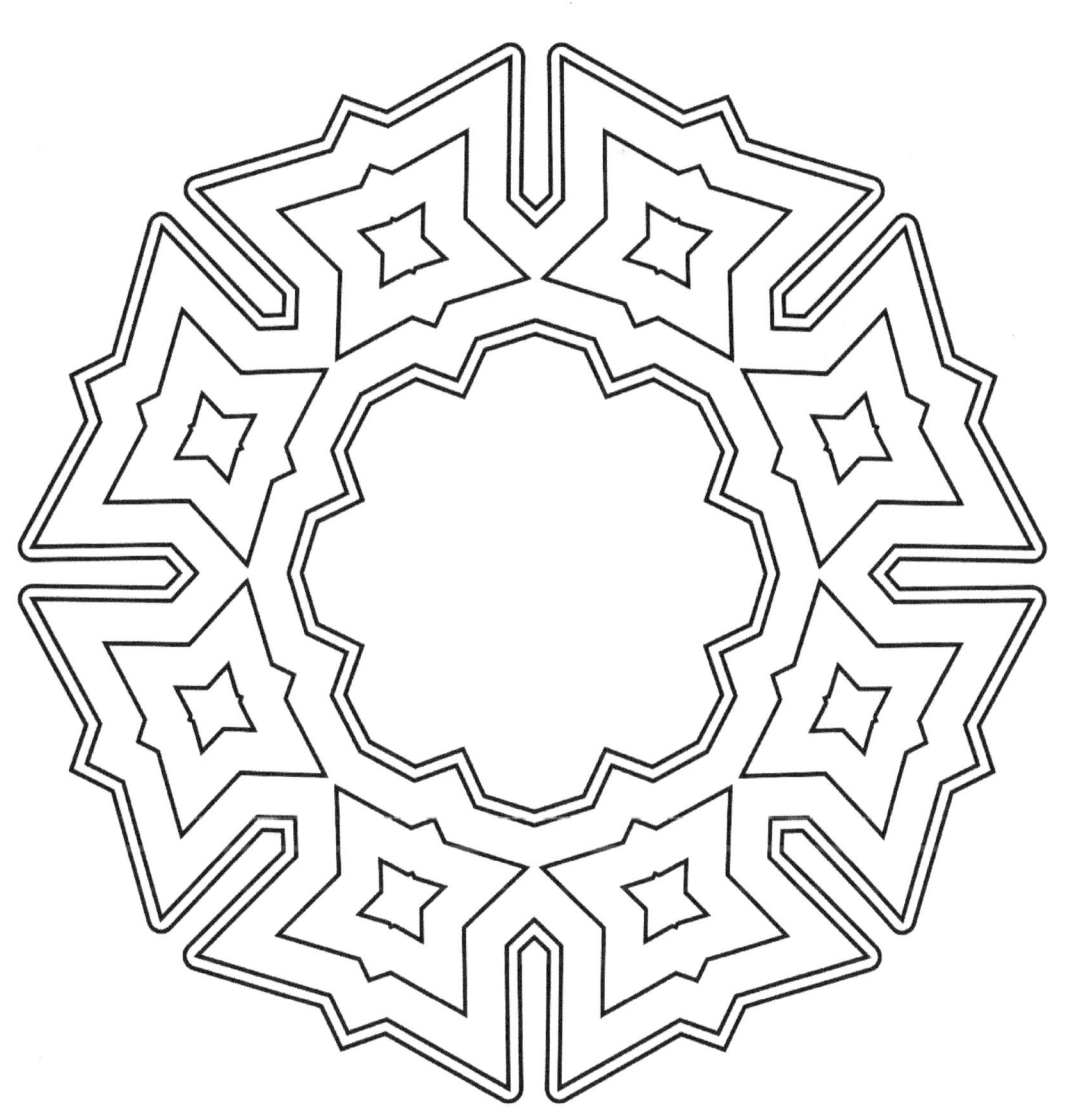

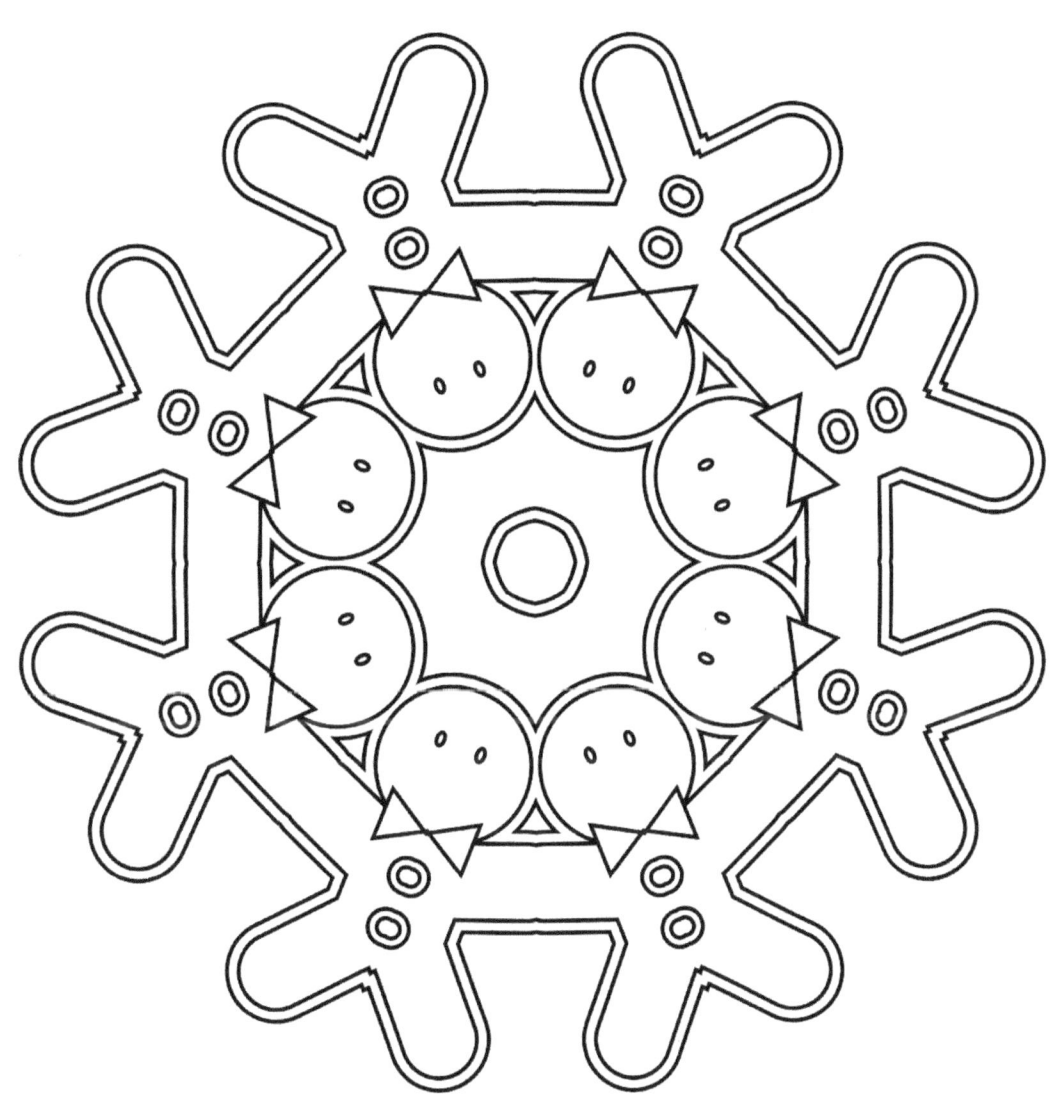

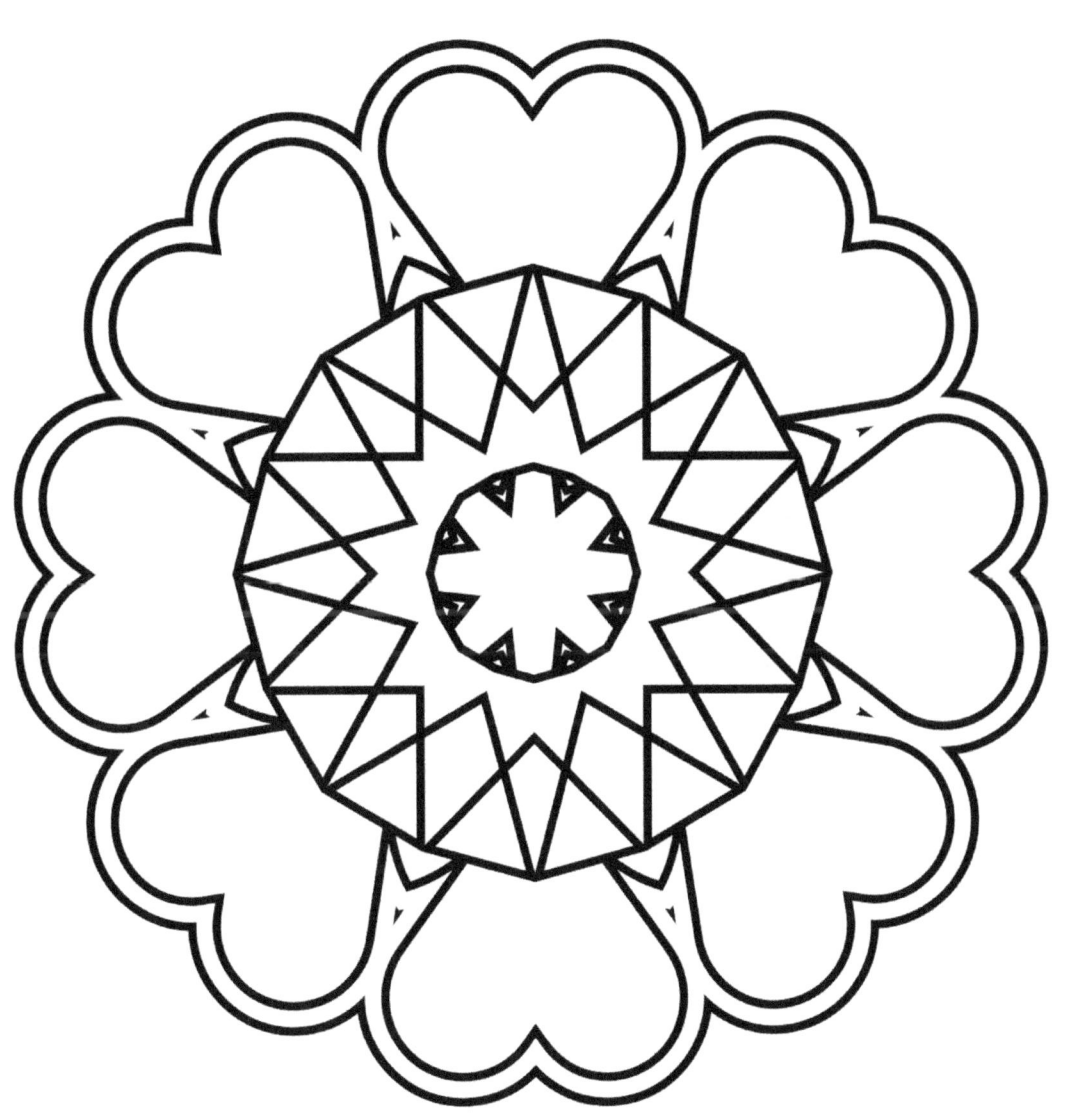

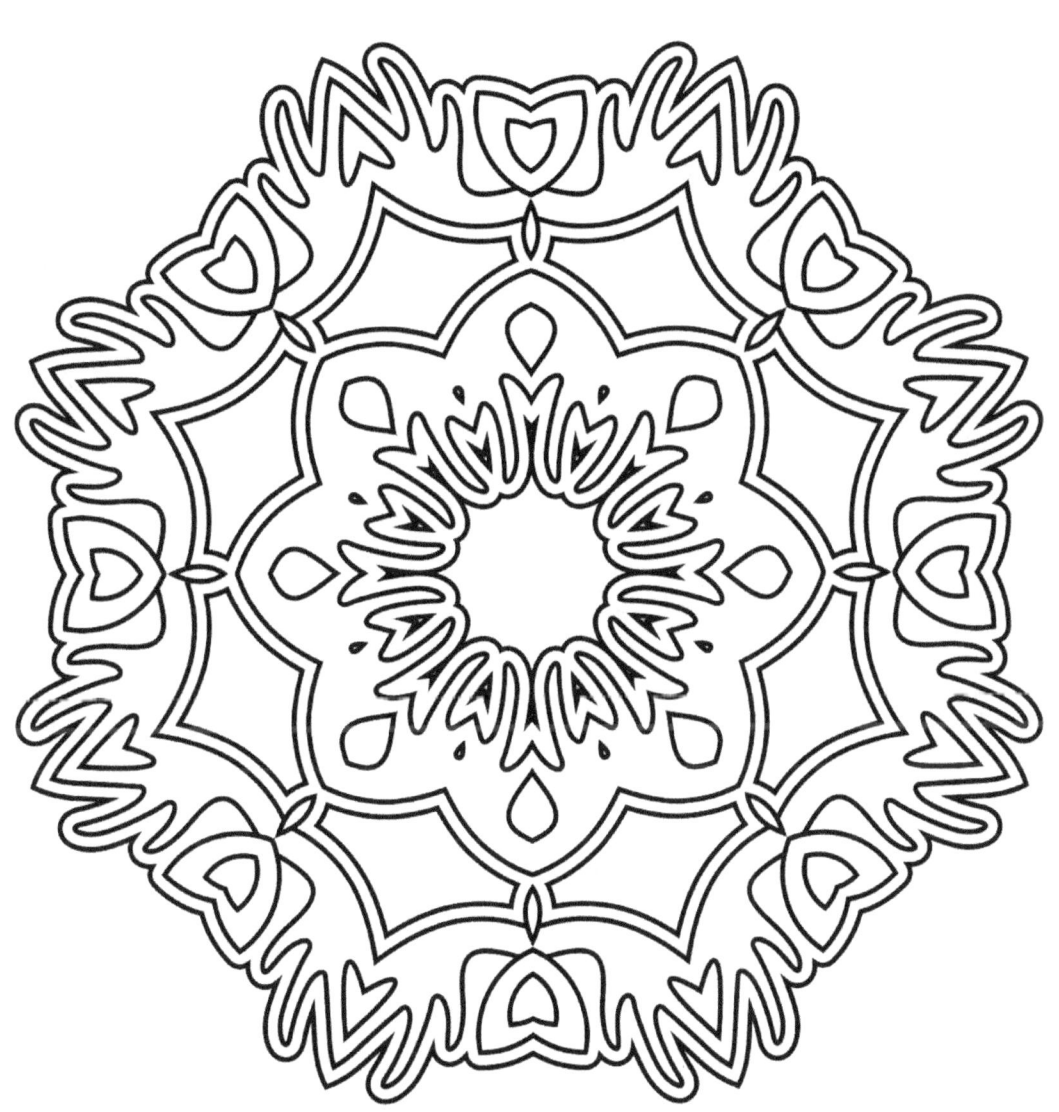

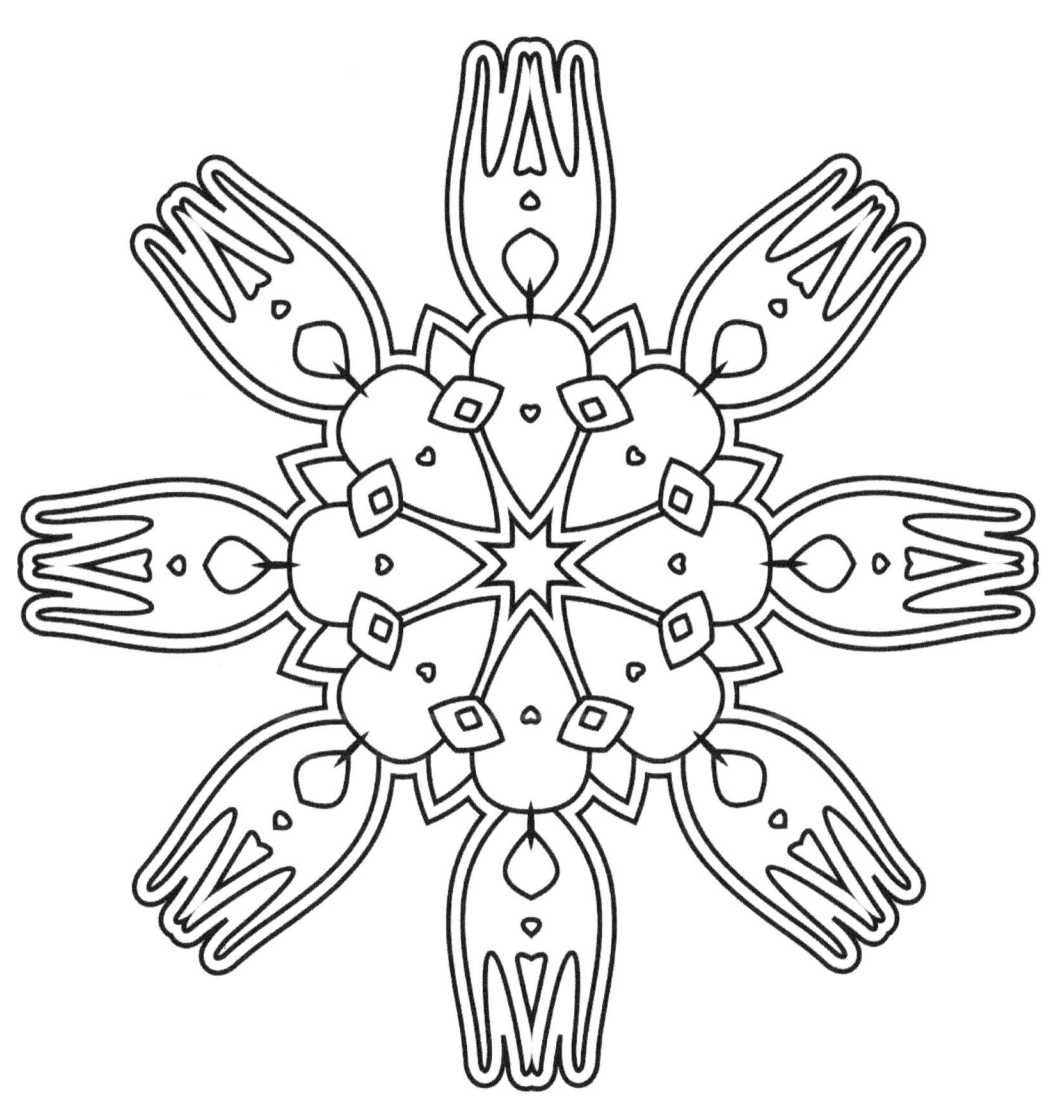

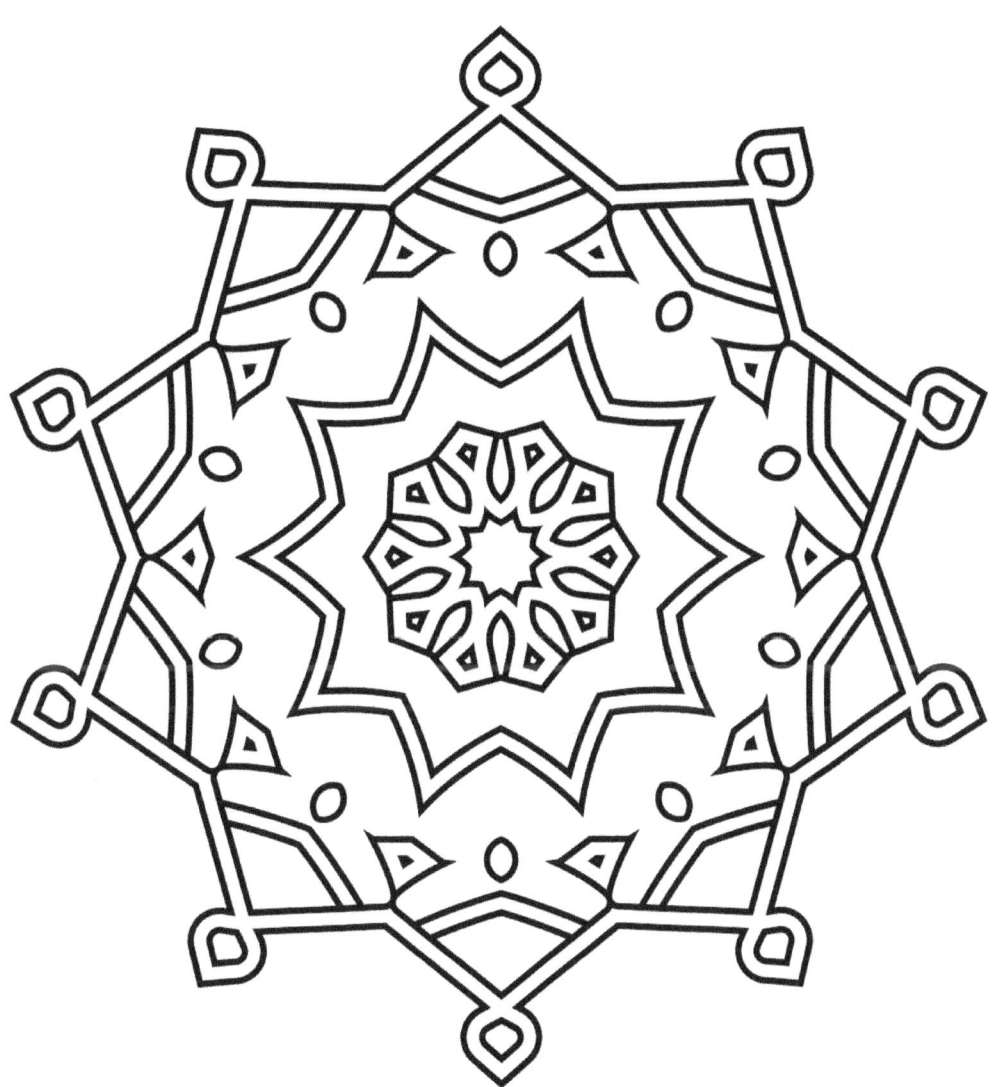

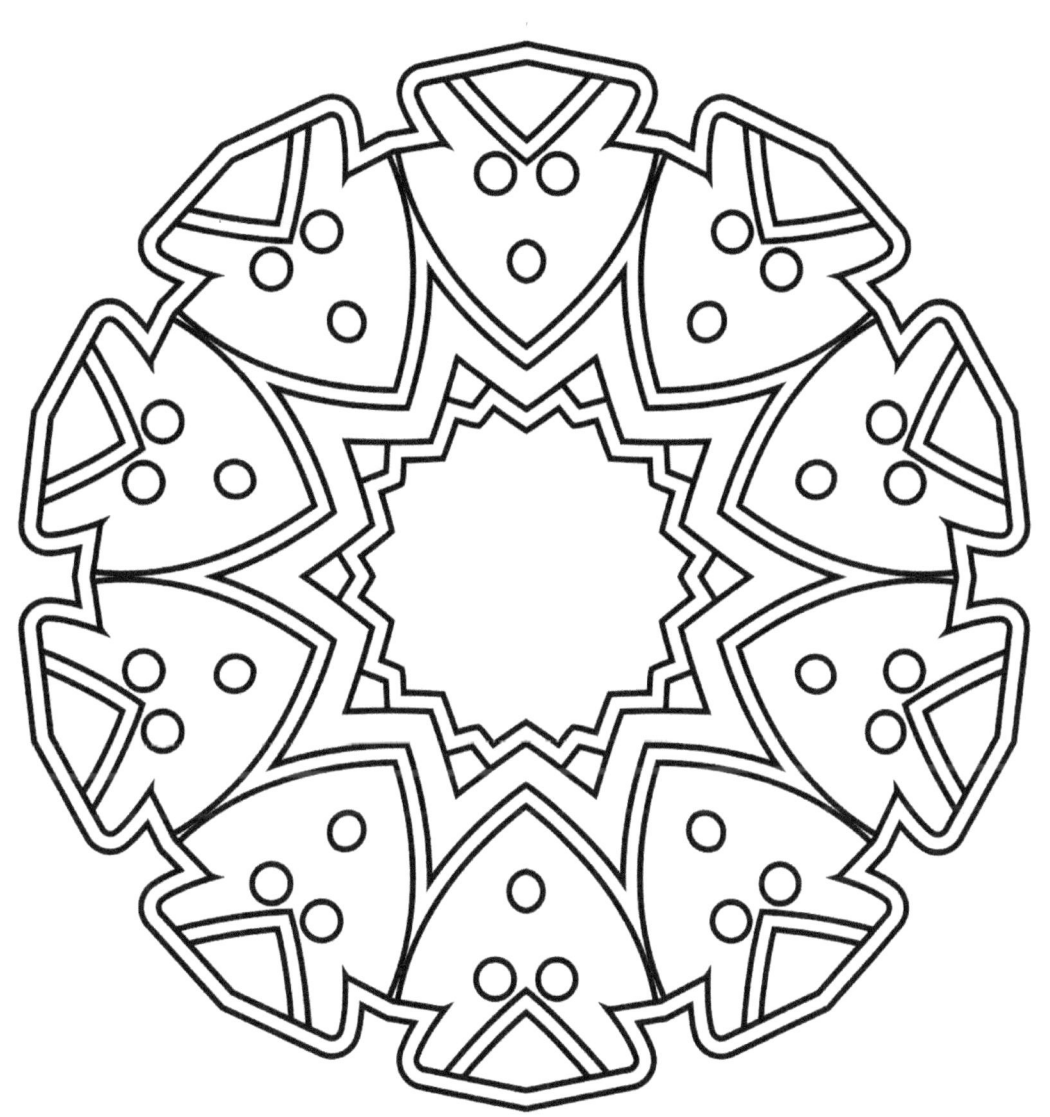

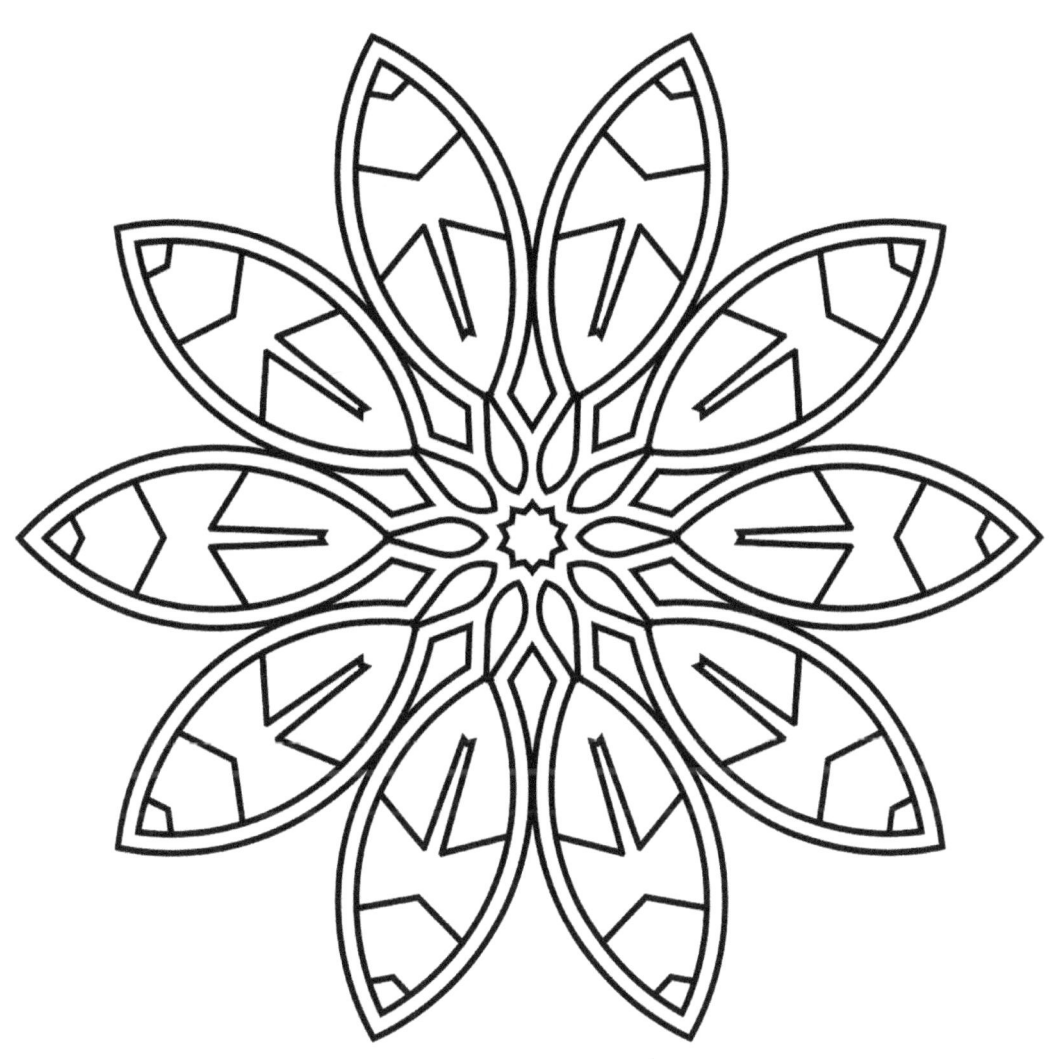

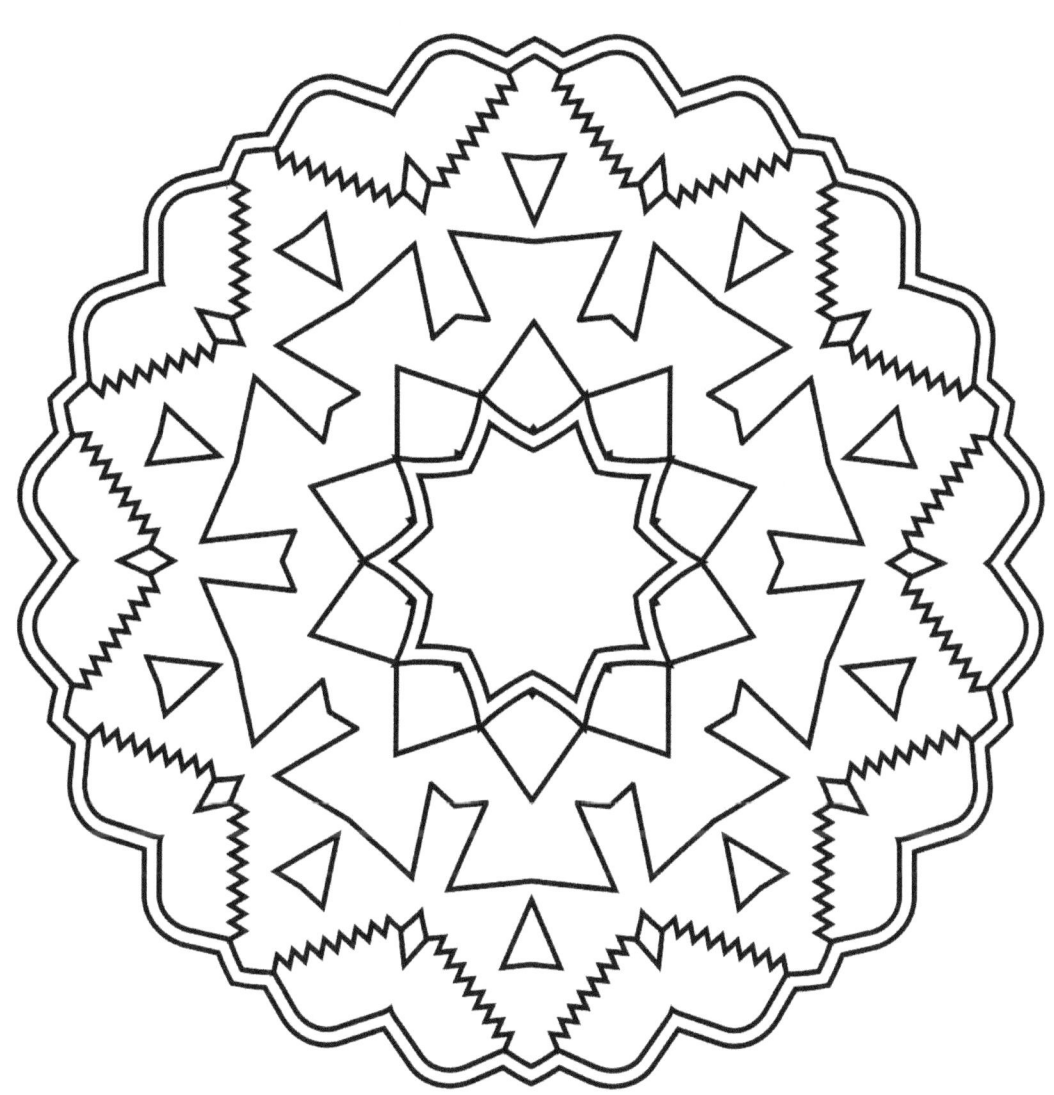

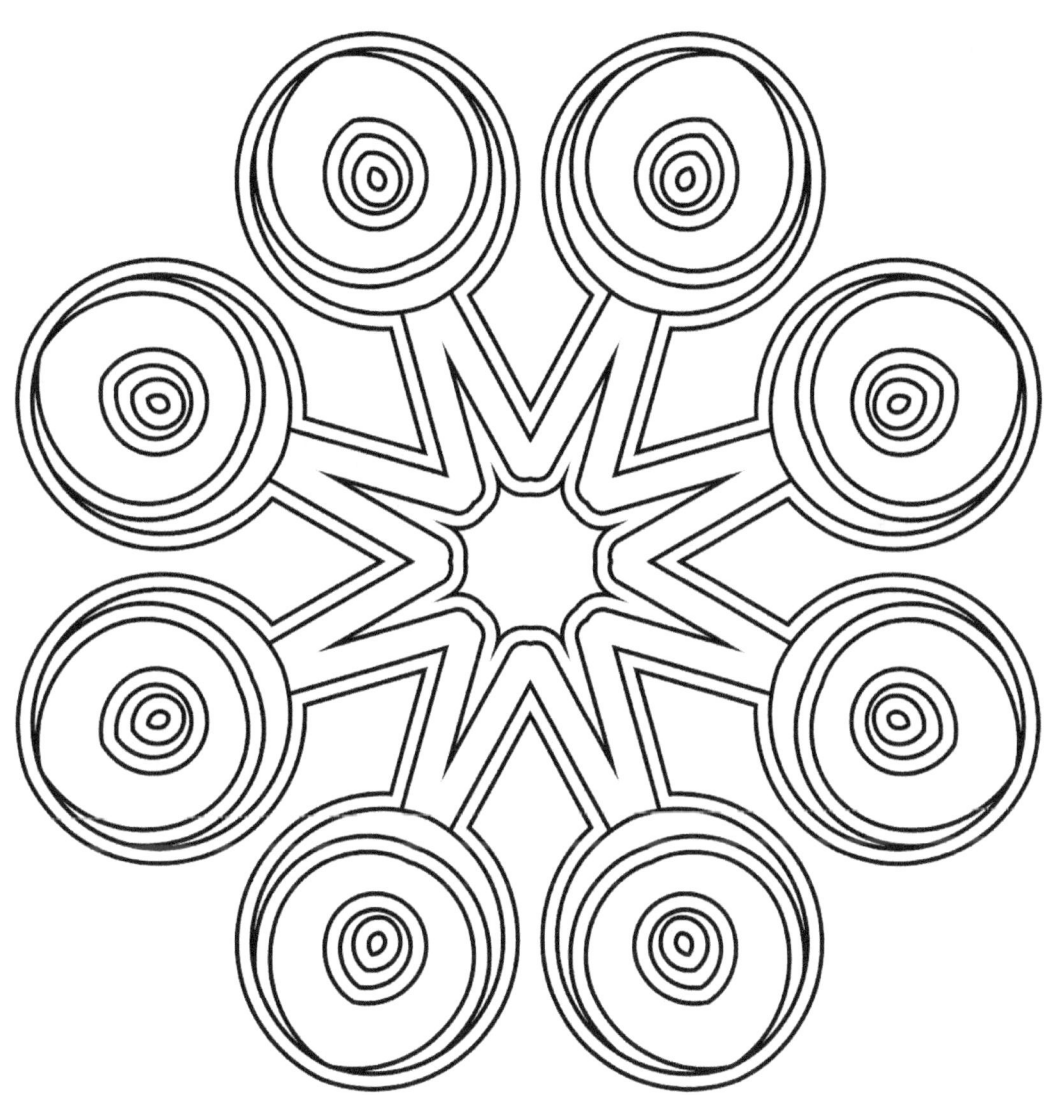

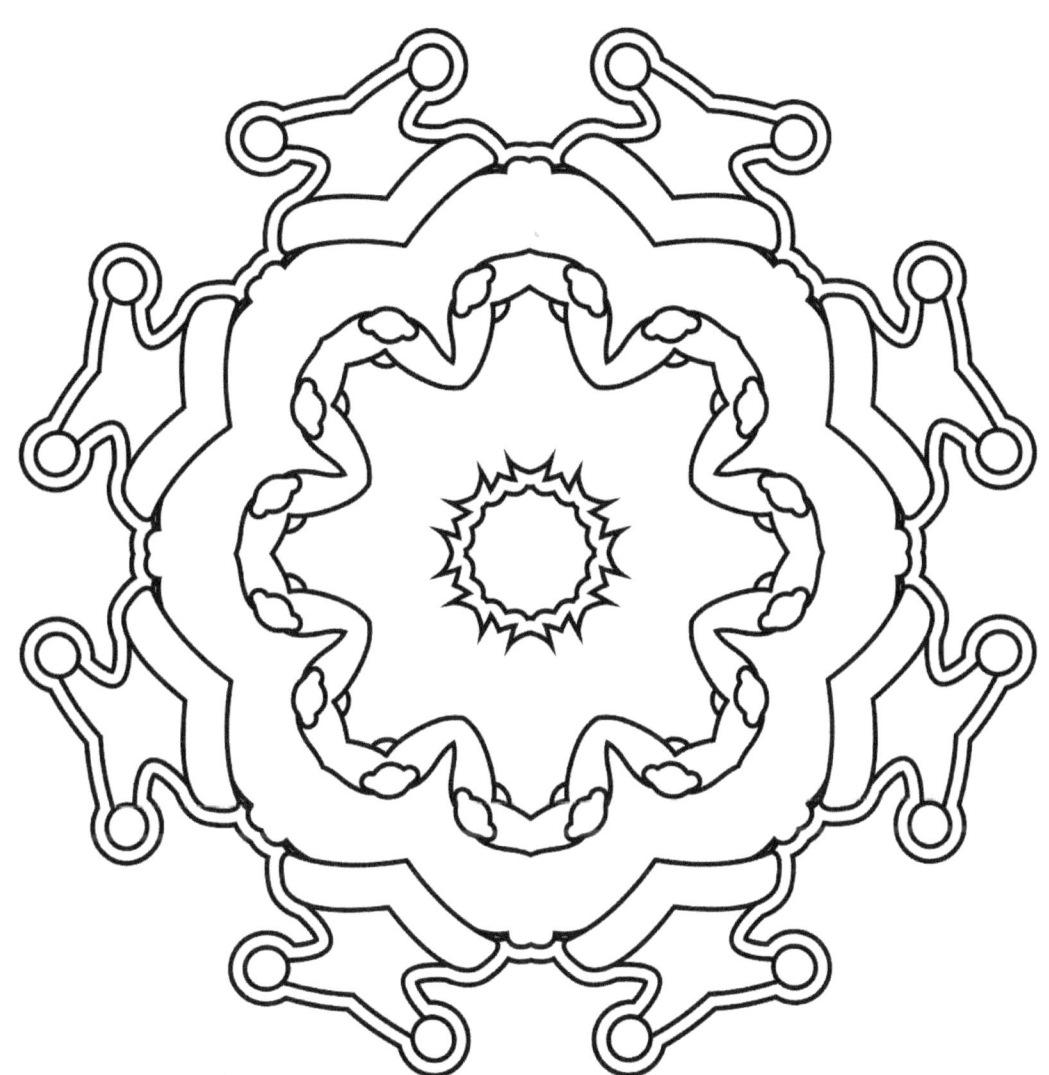

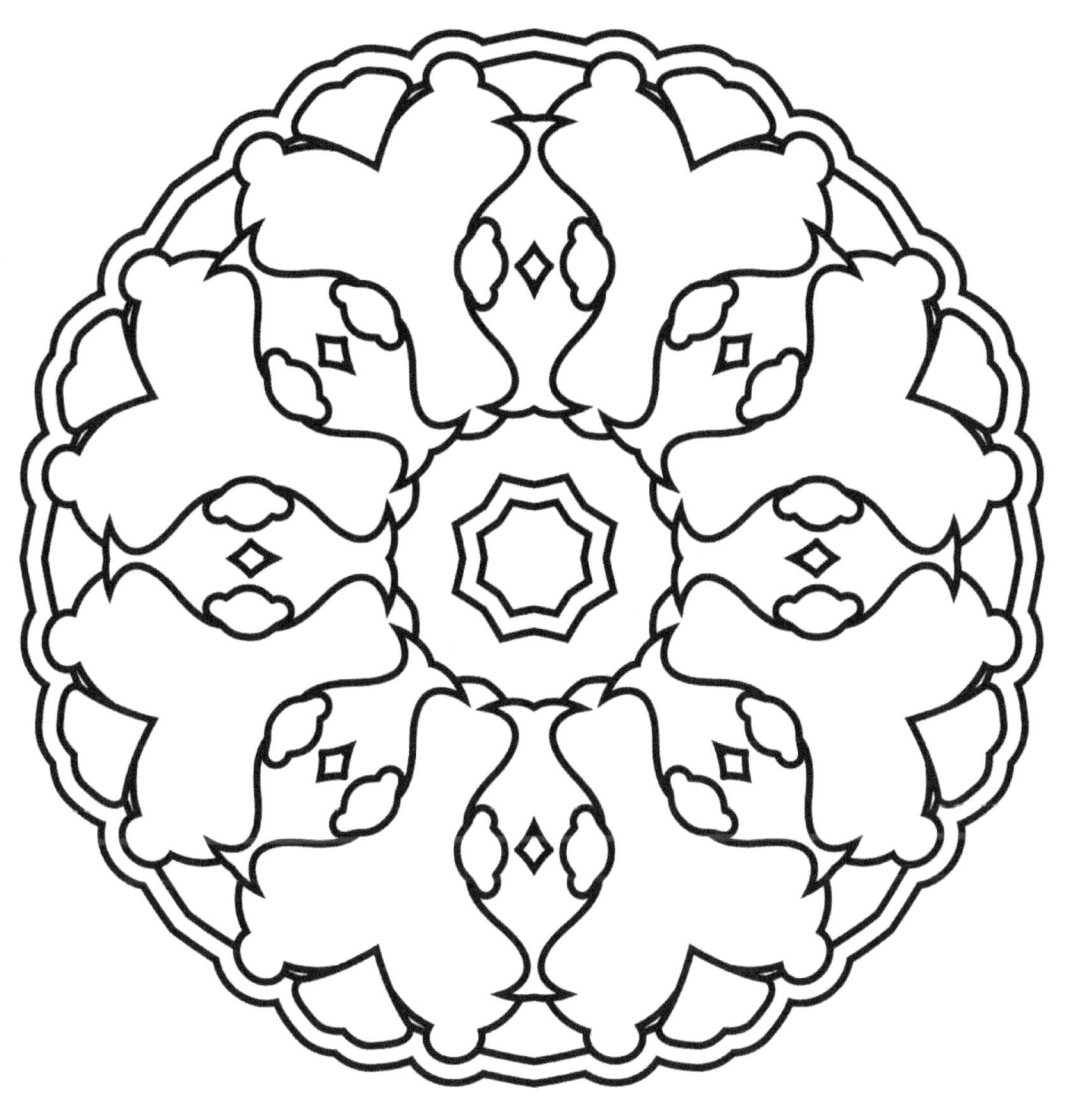

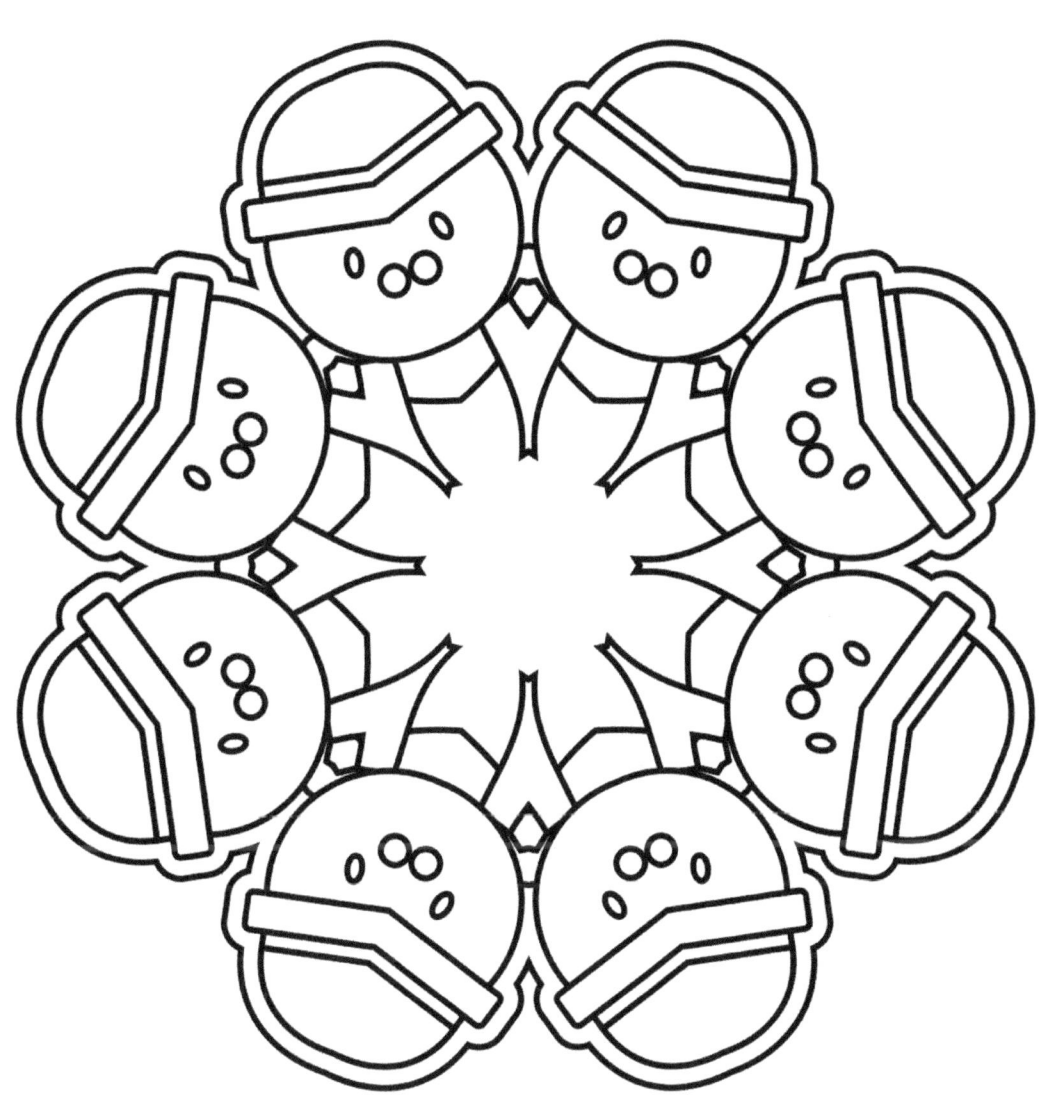

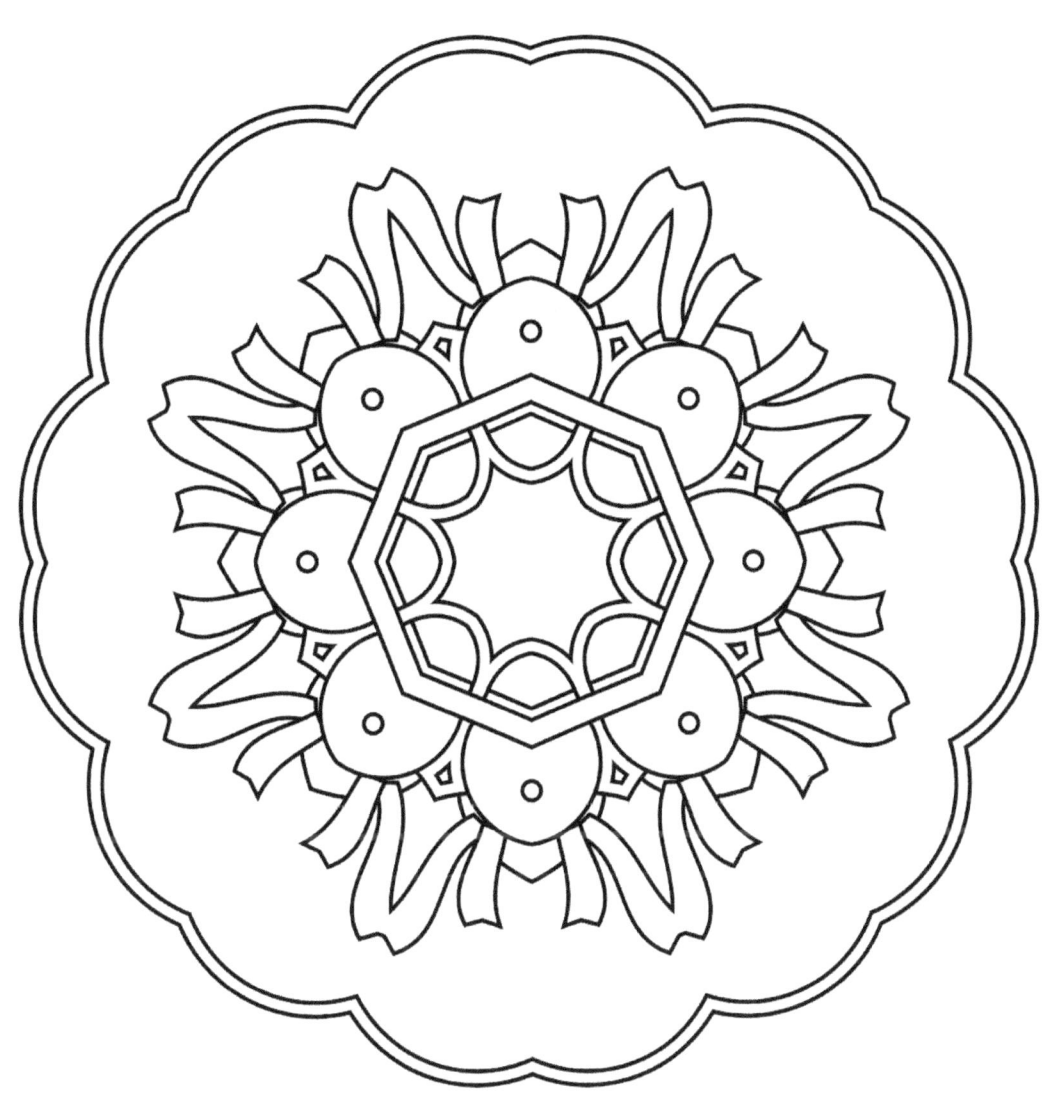

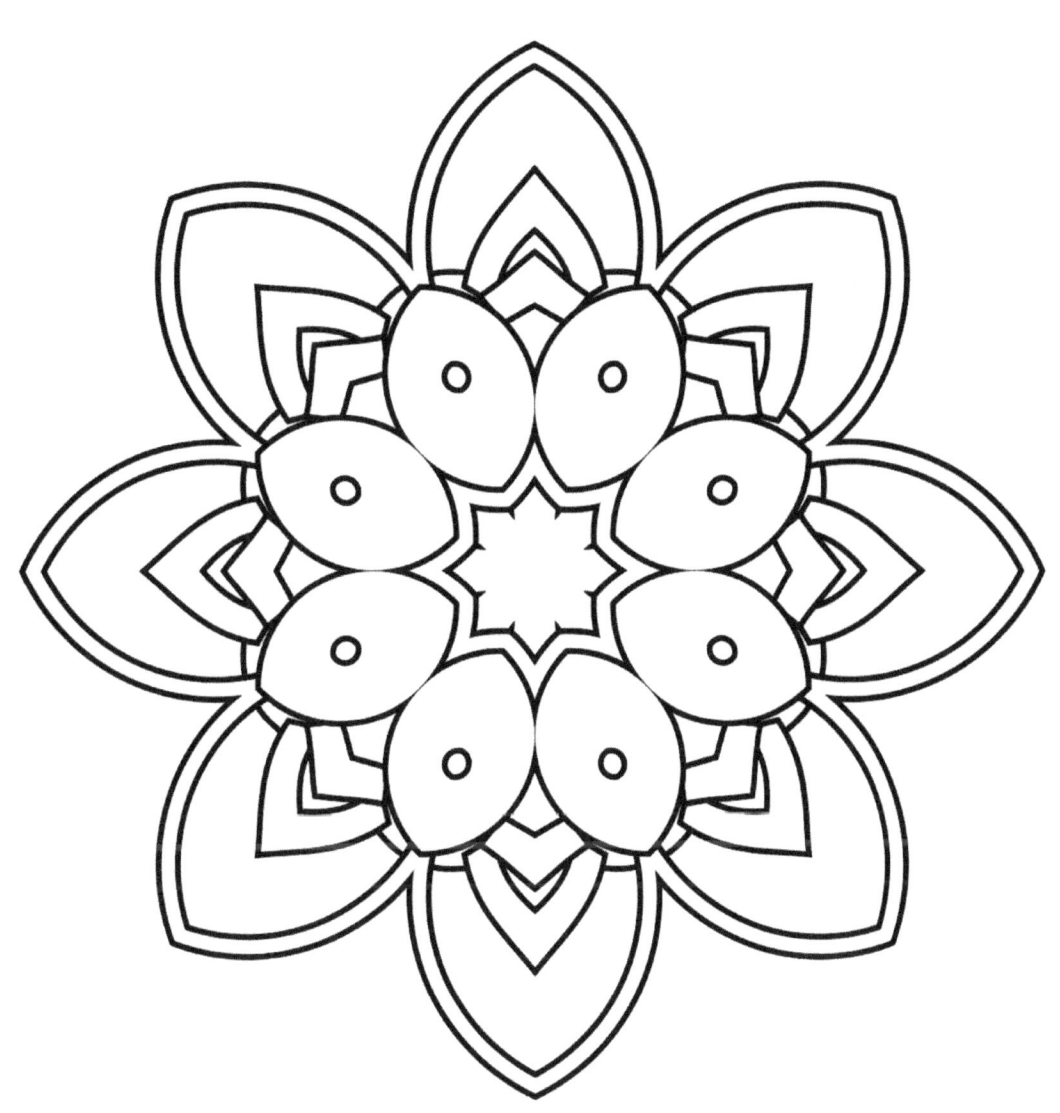

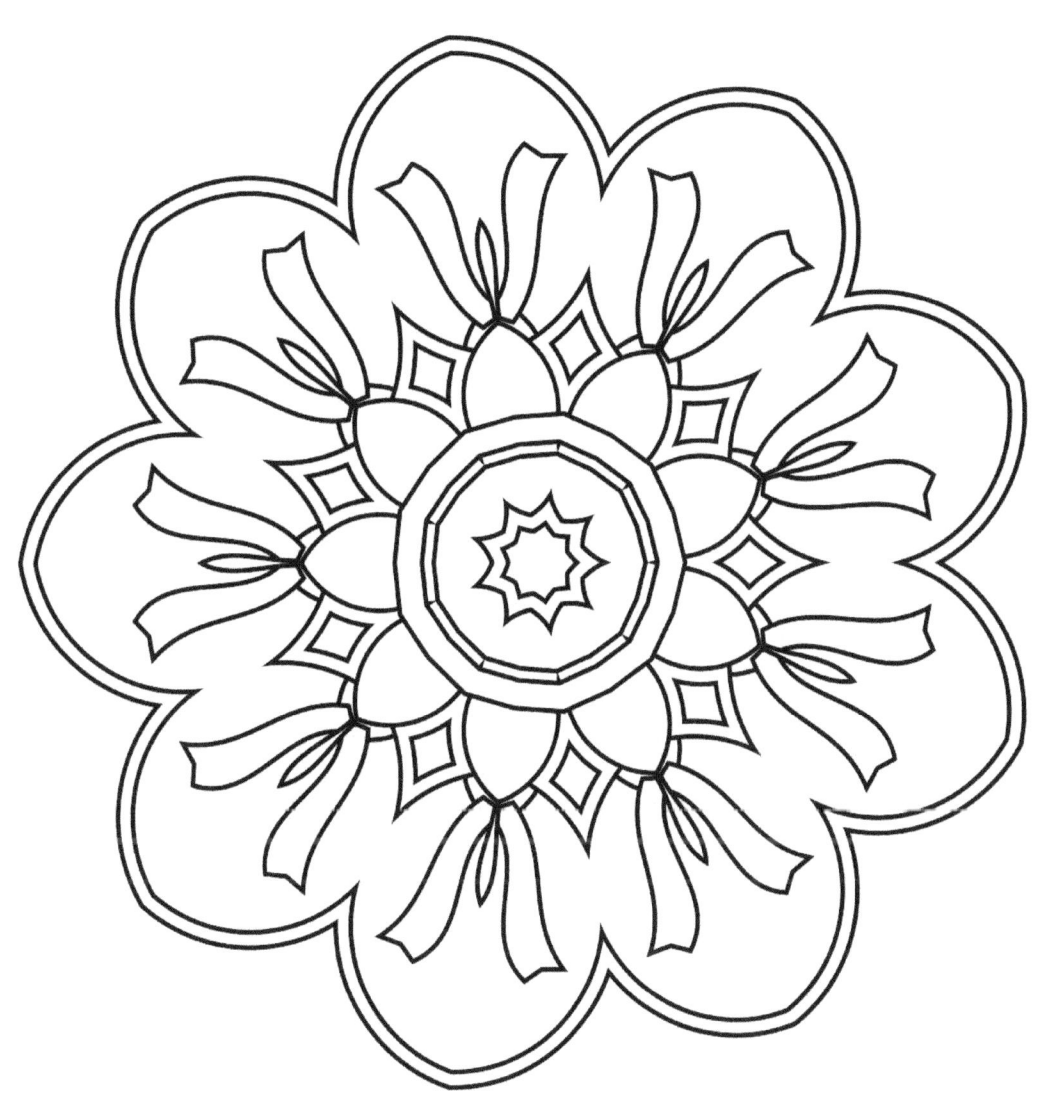

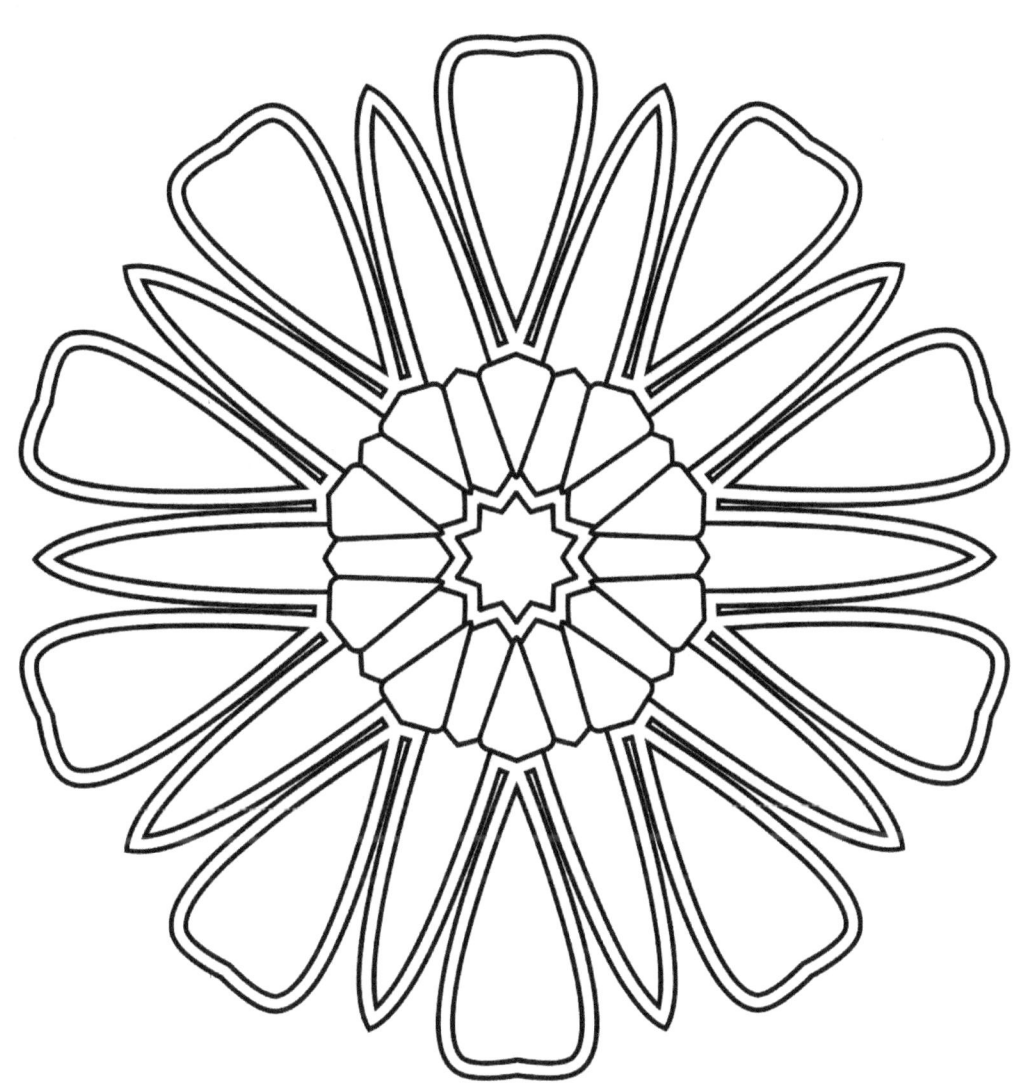

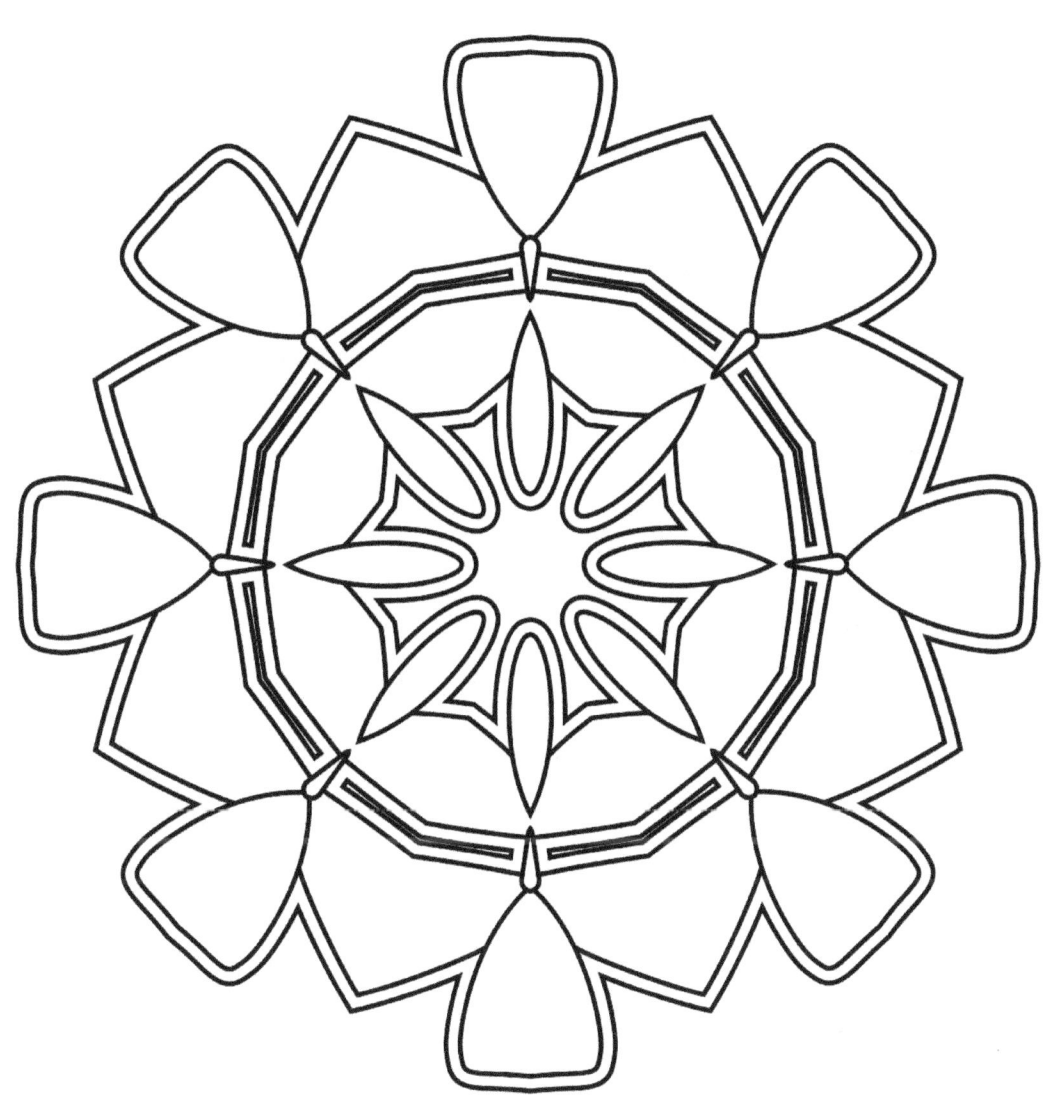

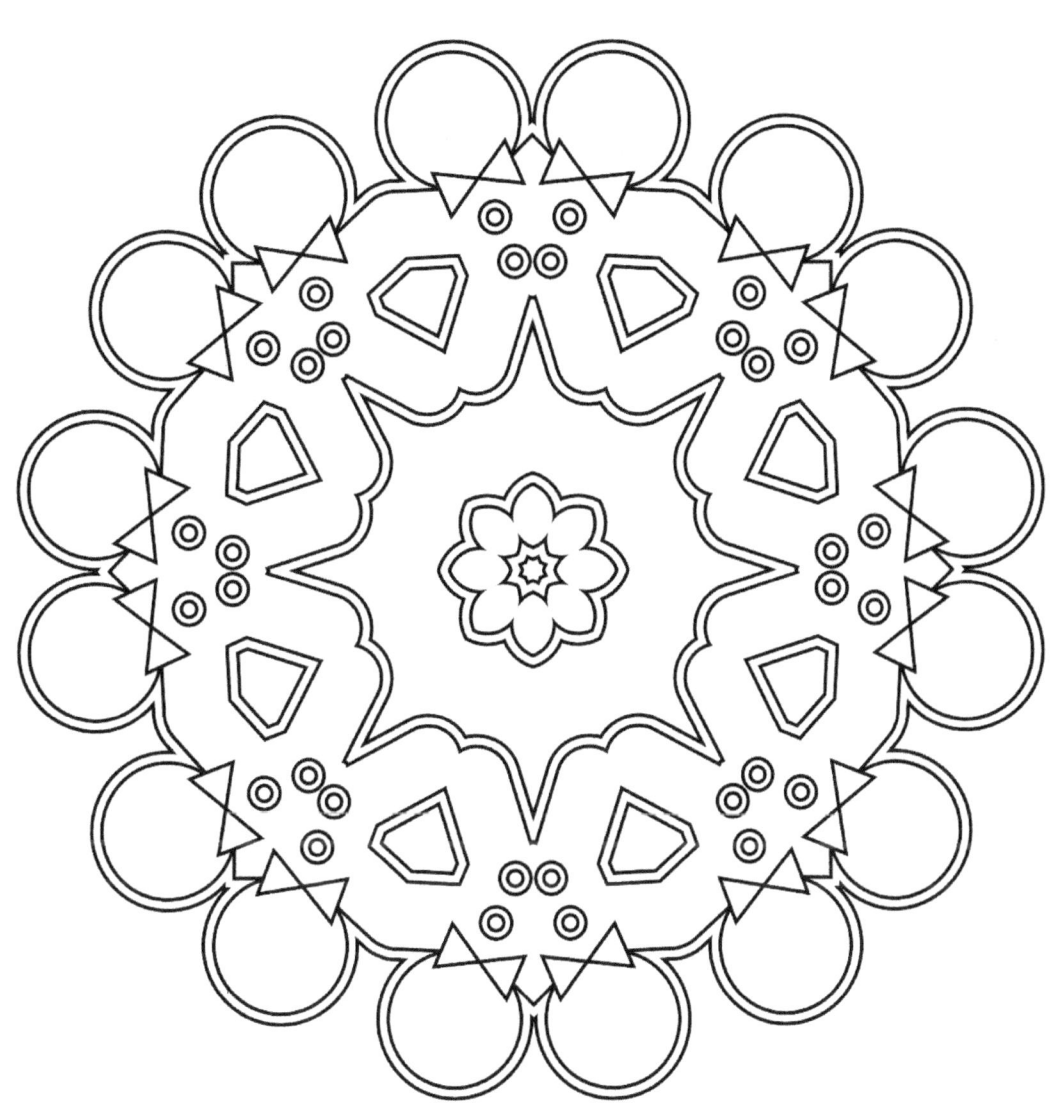

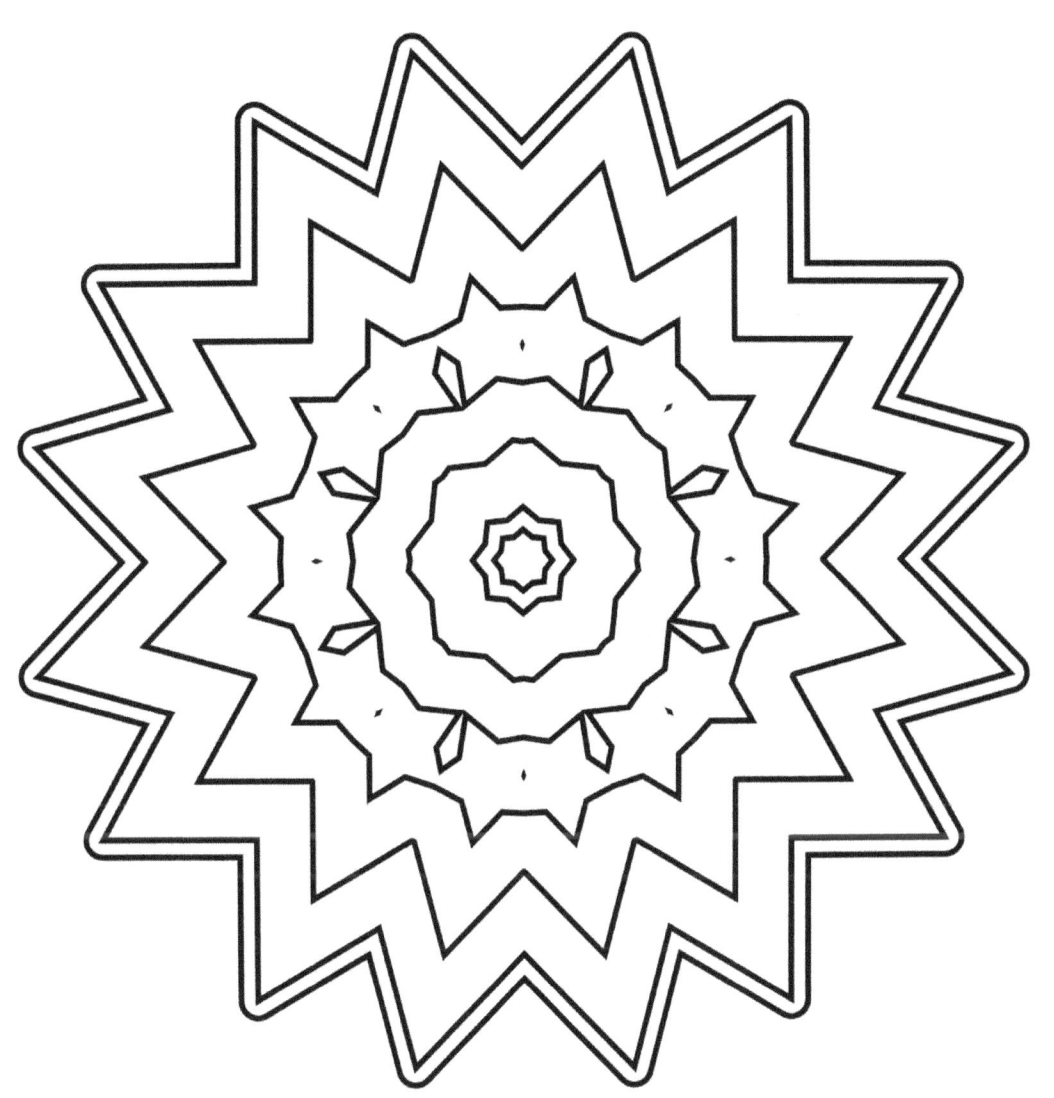

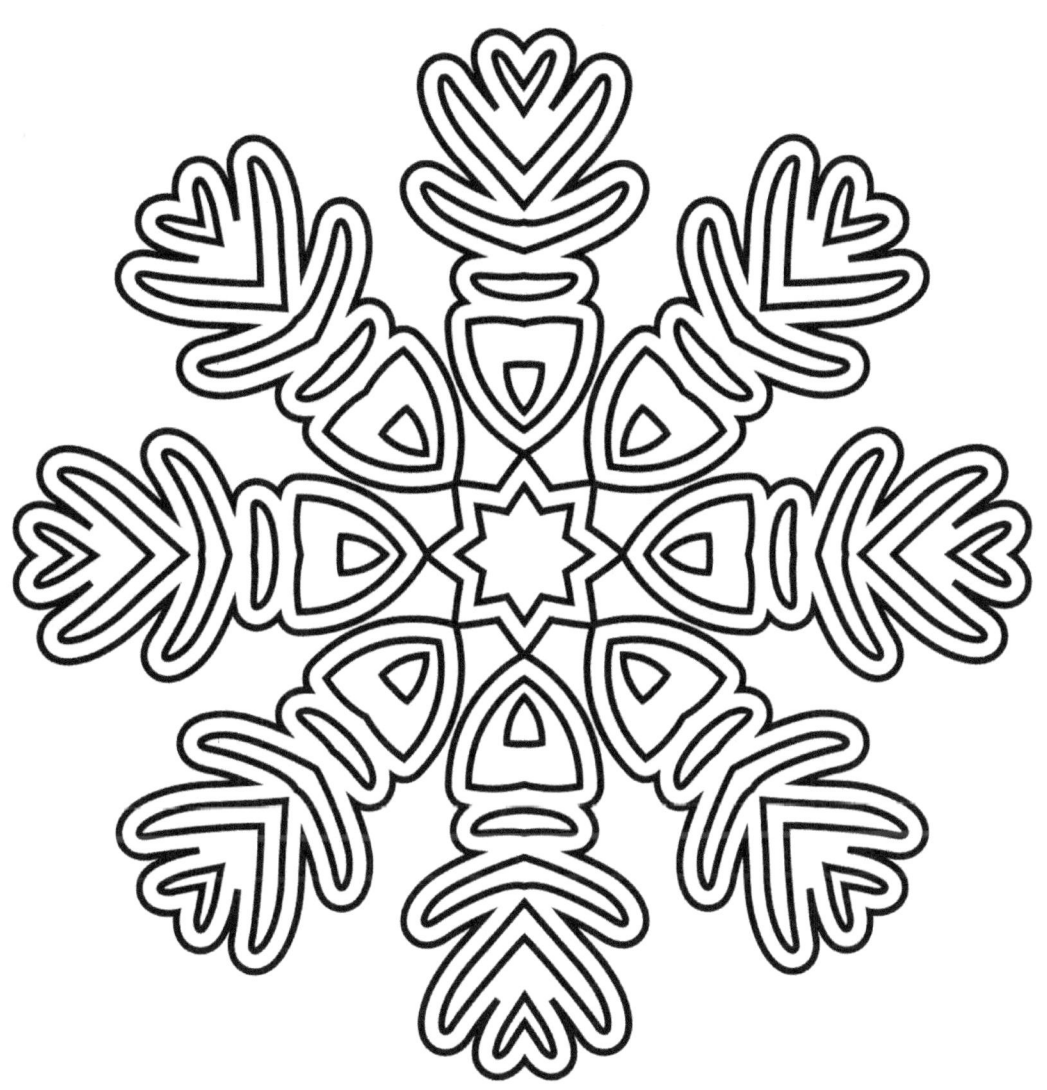

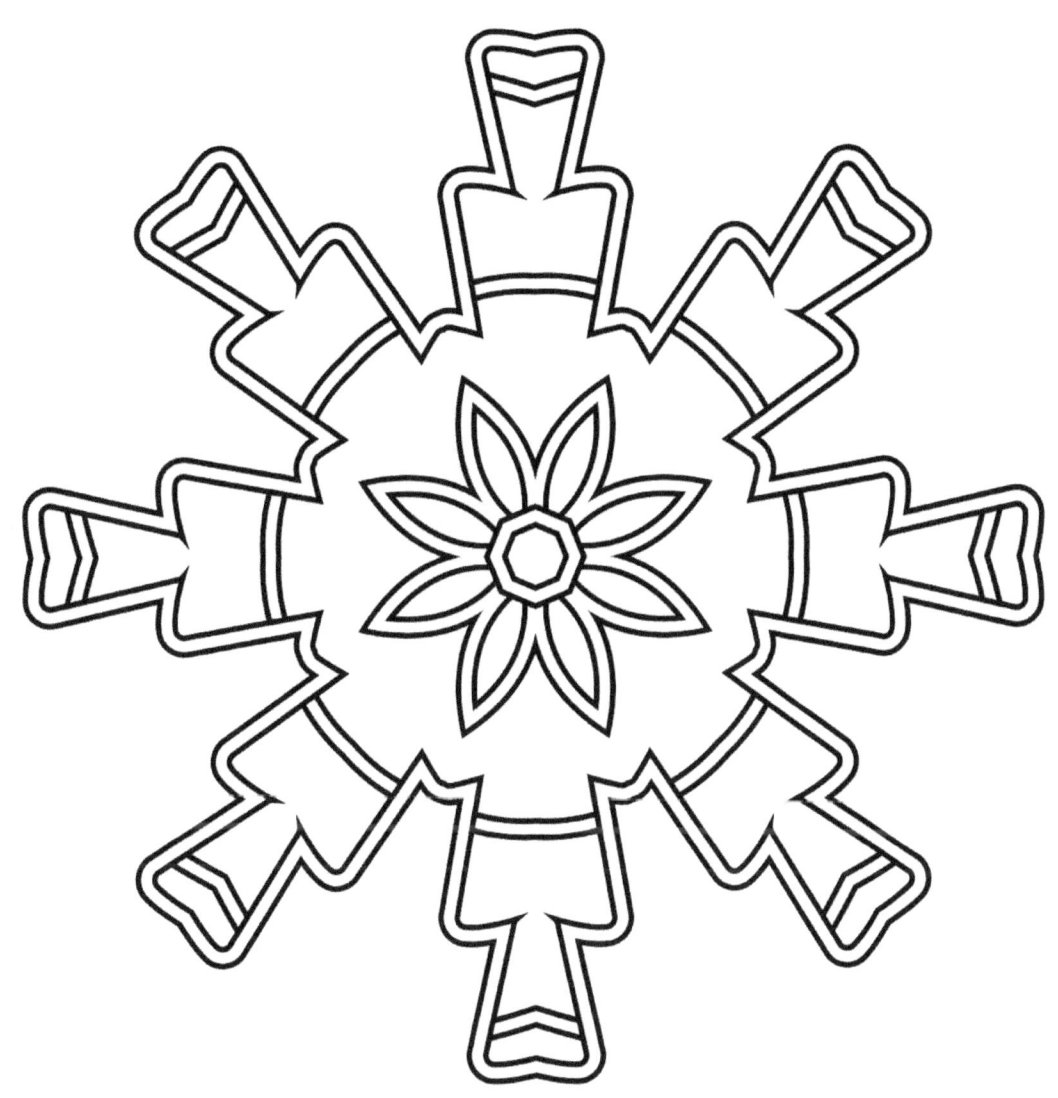

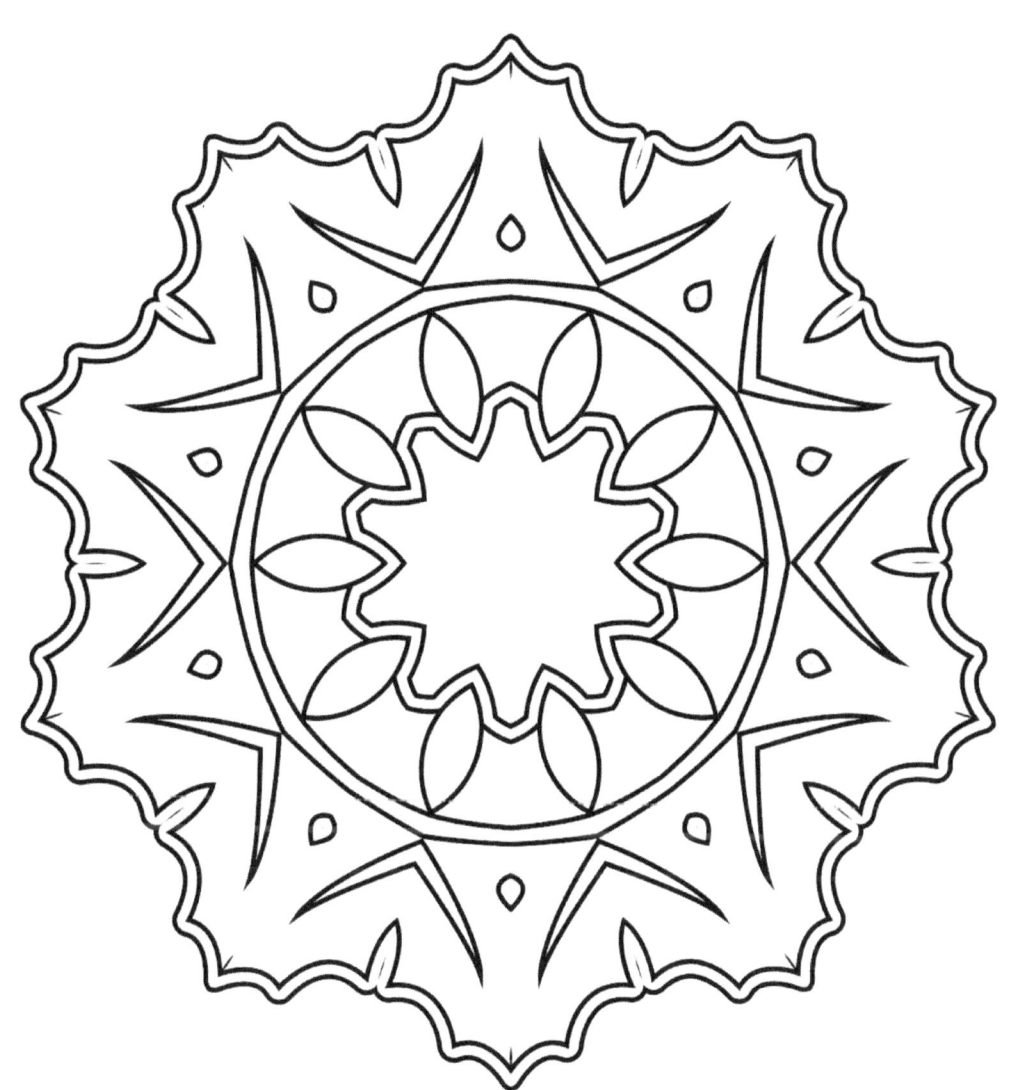

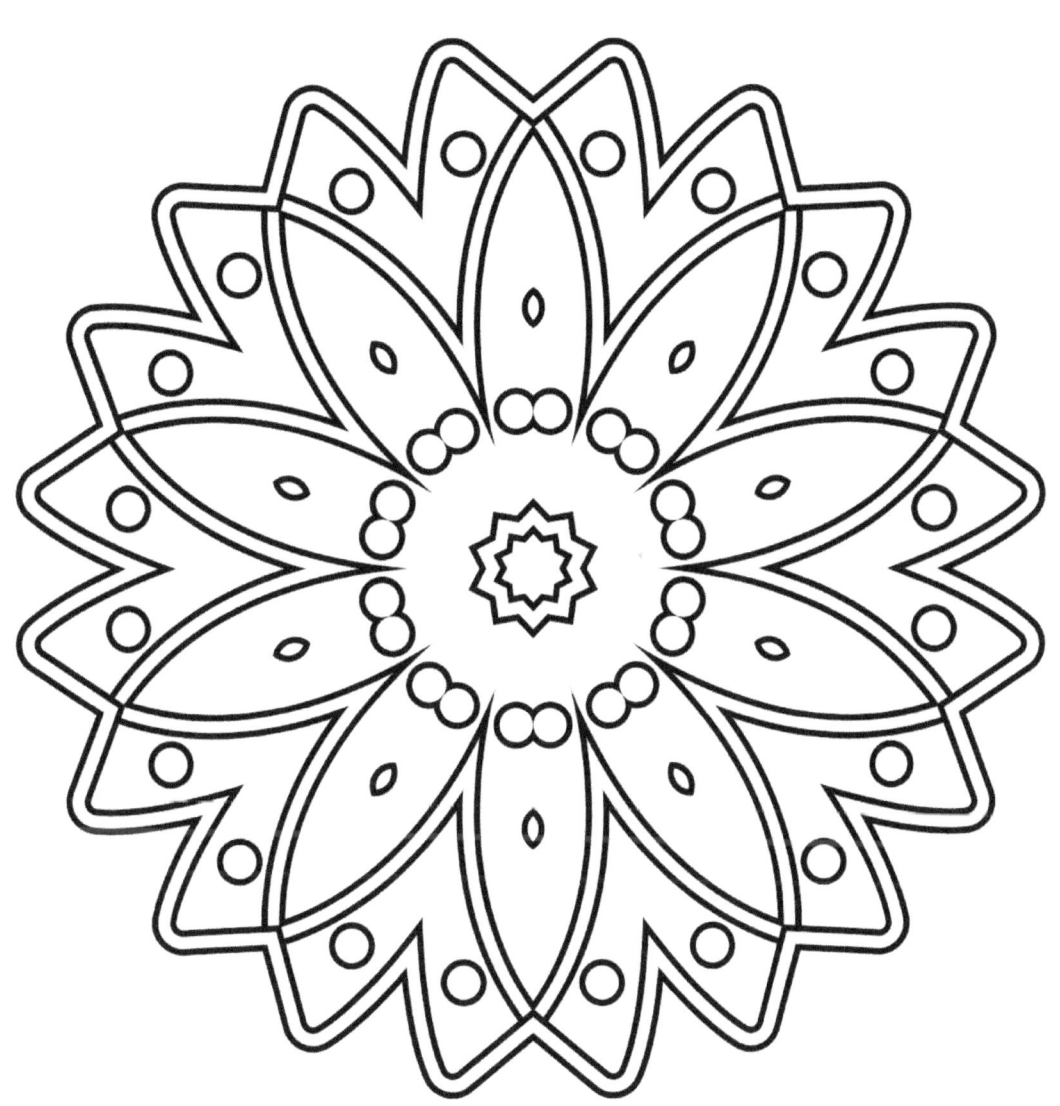

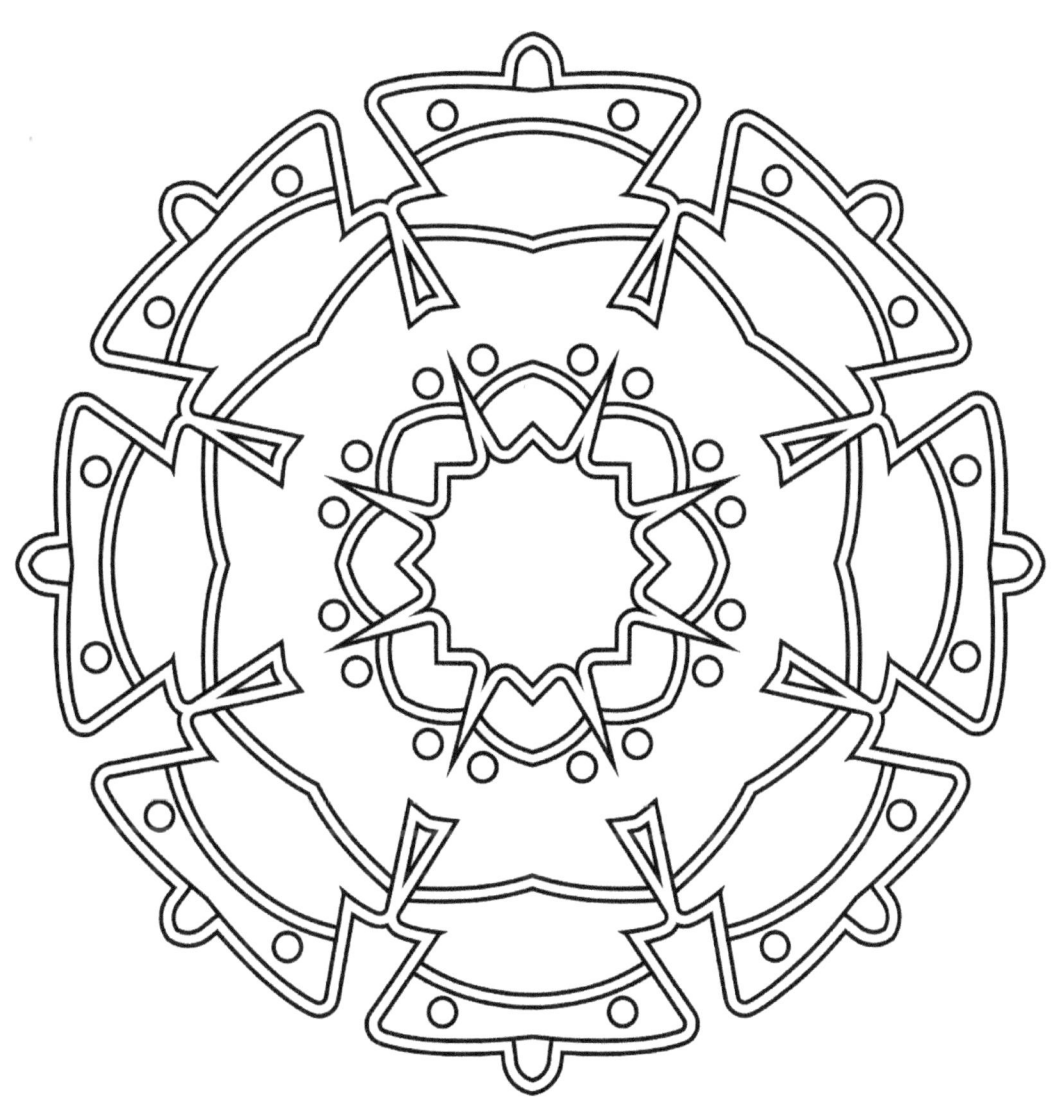

A Note About The Author

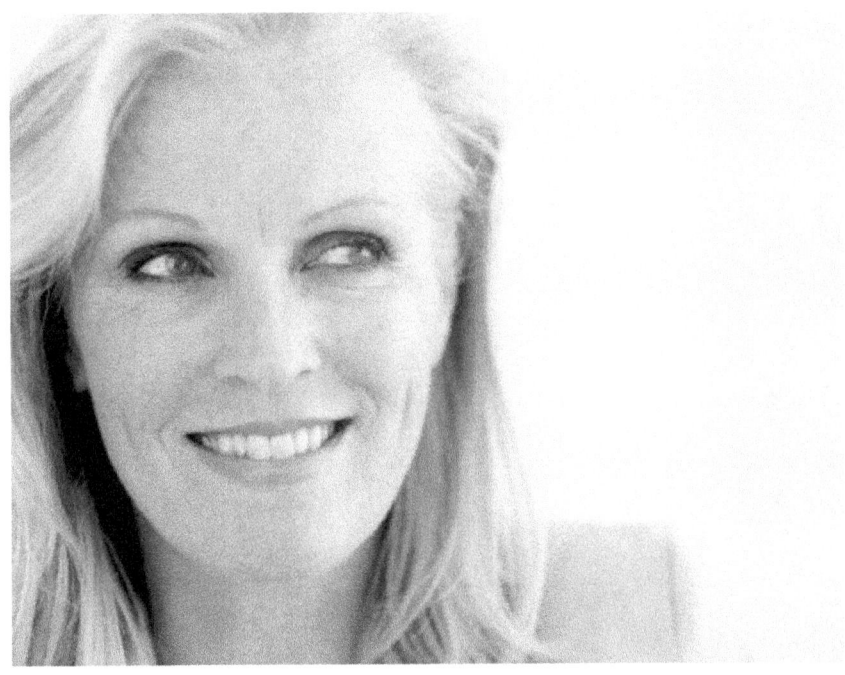

Belinda L. Frazier
Feel free to contact Belinda L. Frazier at belinda.coloring@gmail.com

Check out their Amazon profile here:
http://www.amazon.com/-/e/B01FSO94TA

www.ingramcontent.com/pod-product-compliance
Lightning Source LLC
Chambersburg PA
CBHW080631190526
45169CB00009B/3358